Certificate

of

ADOPTION

THE BOOK BELOW WAS ADOPTED BY:

Emily Romsos

ON THIS 3rd. DAY OF Mar., 199_4 IN
HONOR OF:

BOOK: Austrailian Animals

AUTHOR: Kellie Conforth

A Picture Book of

AUSTRALIAN ANIMALS

Written and Illustrated by Kellie Conforth

Troll Associates

PLATYPUS

The platypus looks like three different animals put together. It has thick brown fur and a flat broad tail like a beaver. Its front paws are webbed like an otter's paws. And its wide bill looks like it belongs on a duck.

The platypus paddles through the water, using its bill to scoop up worms and other small animals that live at the bottom of streams and ponds. Then it stores the food in its cheek pouches and swims to the surface to chew and swallow it.

The platypus makes its home in underground tunnels or burrows. It makes a cozy nest for itself by placing moist leaves and grass on top of the dirt.

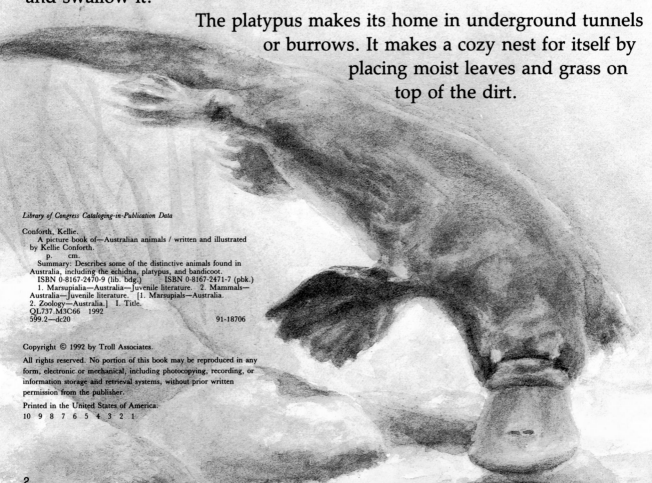

Library of Congress Cataloging-in-Publication Data

Conforth, Kellie.
   A picture book of—Australian animals / written and illustrated by Kellie Conforth.
      p.   cm.
   Summary: Describes some of the distinctive animals found in Australia, including the echidna, platypus, and bandicoot.
   ISBN 0-8167-2470-9 (lib. bdg.)   ISBN 0-8167-2471-7 (pbk.)
   1. Marsupialia—Australia—Juvenile literature.   2. Mammals—Australia—Juvenile literature.   [1. Marsupials—Australia. 2. Zoology—Australia.]   I. Title.
QL737.M3C66   1992
599.2—dc20   91-18706

Printed in the United States of America.
10 9 8 7 6 5 4 3 2 1

ECHIDNA

This spiky animal is also called a *spiny anteater*. It wanders around flicking out its long tongue to lick up a meal of ants and termites. The echidna's slender snout helps it poke through cracks in rotting wood. Here it finds many insects to eat. Using its strong curved claws, it can also rip open termite and ant nests for a tasty meal.

The echidna uses its claws to build an underground nest in the dirt, too. Here the female lays an egg into a pouch on her belly. Ten days later, a baby echidna hatches. The baby will stay in its mother's pouch for the next several weeks while it grows its spines.

KANGAROO

Like all *marsupials* (mar-SOOP-ee-als), kangaroos have built-in body pouches where they raise their young. A baby kangaroo, called a *joey*, stays safe and warm inside the cozy pouch while its mother hops around looking for food. Wherever Mom goes, Baby goes along for the ride. When a baby kangaroo is born, it is only the size of a lima bean. It spends the first months of its life snuggled in the pouch, drinking its mother's milk and growing bigger.

When the joey is big enough, its mother lets the youngster climb out of the pouch for a little play time. As it hops around in the grass, the joey's hind legs become stronger. The kangaroo is a great jumper. Its powerful hind legs push it high off the ground like a pogo stick. And its heavy tail helps the kangaroo keep its balance as it bounces through the fields and plains. There are many kinds of kangaroos, and they come in many different sizes. Eastern gray and red kangaroos are the largest kinds. Full-grown males, called *boomers,* can be up to 7 feet (over 2 meters) tall and weigh as much as 150 pounds (67½ kilograms).

SPOTTED-TAILED QUOLL

The spotted-tailed quoll, or *tiger cat*, hunts both in trees and on the ground. It moves swiftly through the forest, chasing birds, reptiles, and possums, some of its favorite foods. Like the big cats, it has strong, sharp teeth and powerful claws to help catch its prey. But unlike the big cats, the tiger cat is a marsupial.

EASTERN QUOLL

Another type of quoll, the eastern quoll, is only about the size of a house cat. When the young grow too big for their mother's pouch, they cling to her back—even when she goes out at night to hunt for insects to eat.

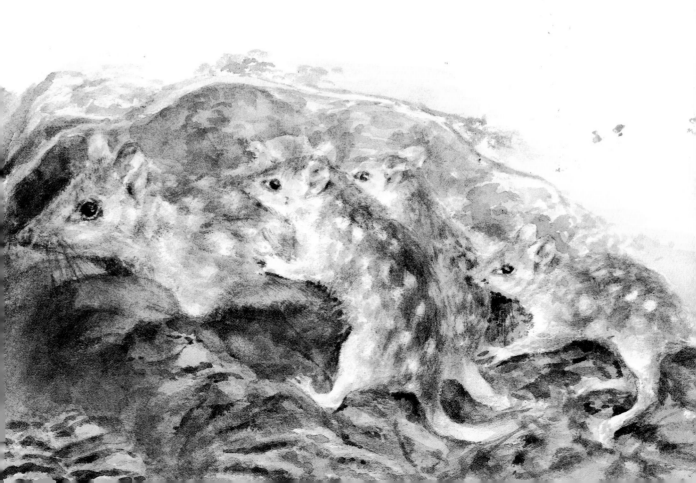

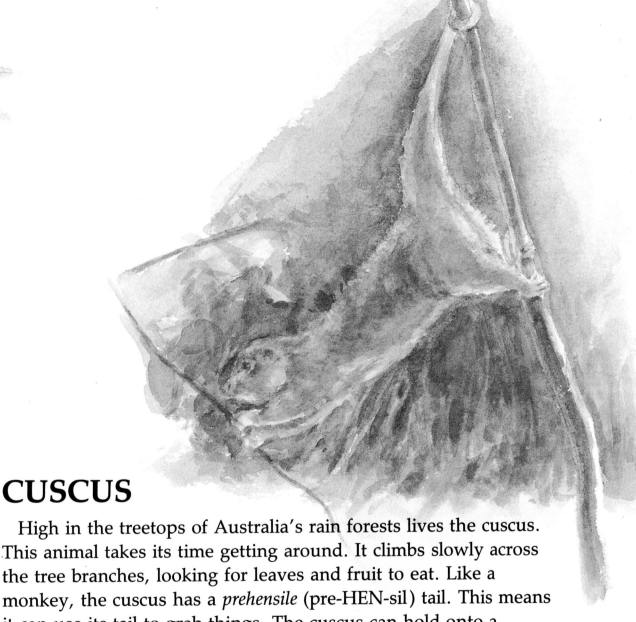

CUSCUS

High in the treetops of Australia's rain forests lives the cuscus. This animal takes its time getting around. It climbs slowly across the tree branches, looking for leaves and fruit to eat. Like a monkey, the cuscus has a *prehensile* (pre-HEN-sil) tail. This means it can use its tail to grab things. The cuscus can hold onto a branch with its tail while using its front paws to pick some delicious berries off a nearby tree.

13

GLIDER

The big-eyed glider gets its name from the graceful way it soars through the air. It cannot fly like birds do, because it does not have wings or feathers. Instead, the glider has loose skin between its front and back legs. When it leaps from a tree-top, this skin stretches out like a parachute and the animal glides to another tree.

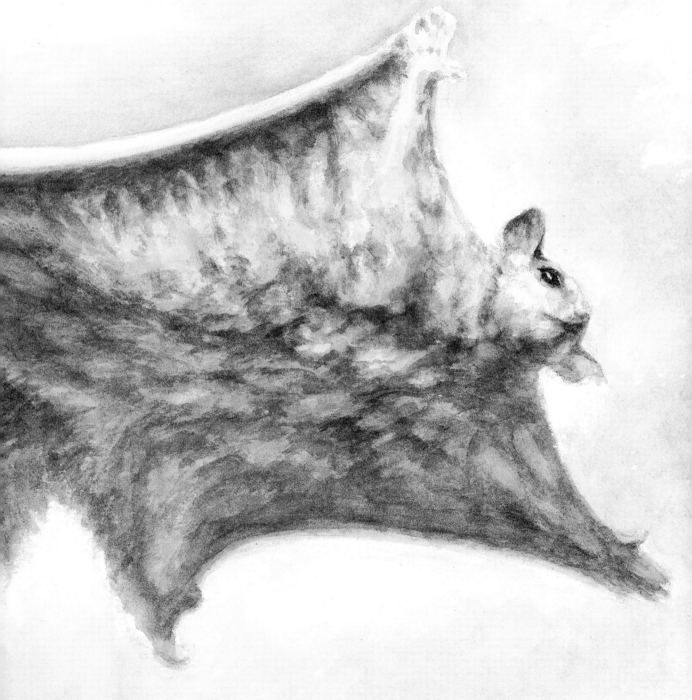

KOALA

The koala spends much of its time munching on the gum leaves and young shoots of the *eucalyptus* (YOO-kah-liptus) tree. This is the only food the koala eats, and Australia is the only continent where these rare trees grow in the wild. This cuddly-looking marsupial likes to sleep through most of the hot day. But as soon as the sun begins to set, the baby koala climbs up on Mom's back. Off they go, collecting leaves to fill their hungry bellies.

NUMBAT

The numbat makes its home in the woodlands of Australia. Here it explores rotting wood and logs to find a meal of termites—its favorite food. A numbat can lick up several hundred termites a second!

This animal's reddish-brown fur is striped with white to match the colors of the woodlands. The numbat is slow-moving and cannot run fast enough to escape from larger animals. By standing very still, the numbat blends into the woods around it so it cannot be seen by dangerous predators.

19

HONEY POSSUM

The honey possum, a tiny marsupial, holds onto the bright blossoms of the banksia plant and licks up nectar and pollen from the flowers. The tip of the honey possum's tongue is prickly, like a brush, so the food sticks to it and is easier for the possum to eat.

EASTERN BARRED BANDICOOT

The bandicoot uses the long claws on its front paws to dig through the dirt. It is looking for earthworms, one of its favorite foods. Most bandicoots nest in shallow holes scooped out of the ground. They sleep during the day, then come out at night to do their hunting.

TASMANIAN DEVIL

This animal lives on an Australian island called Tasmania. The strange howl of this *carnivore,* or meat-eater, gave the Tasmanian devil its name. This animal is mainly a *scavenger*. Instead of killing its food, it usually eats the meat of animals that are already dead. The devil's powerful jaws can crush even very large bones.

WOMBAT

The shy wombat comes out of its burrow at night to nibble grass and roots. It has strong teeth and sharp claws. During the day, the wombat sleeps in its burrow, curled up in a nest made of grass and bark.

DATE DUE

10			
JAN 17 79			
MAY			
S			
O			
MA			
DE			
FE			
A			
O